Contents

Acknowledgements
Text by Deryk Brown.
The publishers would like to thank
Winmau for their photographic
contribution to this book.

Photographs on the outside covers and on
pages 19, 22, 23, 25, 27, 28, 29 and 30
courtesy of Allsport (UK) Ltd.
All other photographs by Steve Daszko.
Illustrations by 1–11 lineart.

Note   Throughout the book players
and officials are referred to individually
as 'he'. This should, of course, be taken
to mean 'he or she' where appropriate.

Foreword

Darts is not only established as one of
the most popular sports in Britain and
the world, but it is also continuing to
develop and progress. New young talent
is coming through at club and county
level and progressing to national, international and world excellence. It is also
noticeable that darts is increasing its
appeal to women, who now account for
some 25% of British players.

It is both encouraging and exciting
that darts has developed greatly in the
last three decades and, as the governing
body of darts in this country, the BDO is
proud to represent over 25,000 British
darts players in all 63 counties nation-
wide. In addition, as a member body of
the World Darts Federation (WDF), the
BDO is part of a darts 'family' of
500,000 players in 53 countries
throughout the world.

It is wonderful to be a part of such an
exciting era in British and world darts.
The BDO is not only delighted that more
and more young people are coming into
the sport, but also greatly encouraged
by their commitment and playing stan-
dards. Of course, we still have many
talented experienced players, but it is
evident that the average age of successful players is getting younger, and
scoring averages are getting higher at
all levels.

It augurs well for the sport of darts as
more and more people are encouraged
to take it up from the earliest age possible. That's why this publication is so
valuable for those who want to get to
know the sport. It answers questions
and provides wonderful help to those
just starting to play, as well as providing
tips and information for the more
experienced players.

There is something for everyone
within these pages and the BDO and
WDF executives are delighted to lend
their support to it.

**Olly Croft, Hon. General Secretary,
British Darts Organisation,
World Darts Federation**

Introduction

Darts is a popular game. Very few people have not thrown a dart at some time or other, and large numbers play in public houses, in clubs and in bars on a regular basis. It is an easy game to play, but a hard game to play *well*. As in golf, the margin between success and failure is often tantalisingly small. That is one of the reasons why darts, which began as an English pub pastime, has spread round the world.

Today some 50 nations are members of the World Darts Federation. They include former Communist countries such as Bulgaria, Hungary, Russia and Slovakia, giants such as South Africa, and minnows such as the Faroe Islands. All round the world open tournaments are held.

We have referred to darts as a game rather than as a sport. Most enthusiasts will claim that darts is a sport. They will argue that it requires a wide range of attributes: skill and accuracy; co-ordination between hand and eye; composure and self-discipline; stamina; the mental agility to ensure you do not waste a dart as you work down to a finishing double. Whatever the answer, modern darts is certainly very well organised, very sporting and very demanding.

Useful addresses

British Darts Organisation
2 Pages Lane
Muswell Hill
London
N10 1PS

World Darts Federation
47 Creighton Avenue
Muswell Hill
London
N10 1NR

Darts World (magazine)
9 Kelsey Park Road
Beckenham
Kent
BR3 2LH

The officials

Every local league needs a secretary. The BDO runs a national league containing some 60 counties, all of which need officials. Of course, a major tournament needs skilled hands and brains to run it smoothly.

The two most glamorous jobs are that of the 'MC' and of the 'referee' or 'caller'. The same person may perform both jobs but there are two different functions. The MC introduces the players, gives the sponsor a generous mention, and thanks all those who need to be thanked. The referee or caller is the official who shouts '180!' He has to work out in a split second how many the player has scored. He calls that score and notes that the markers on either side of the dartboard have recorded it correctly and made a correct subtraction. Once the player is on an out shot, the referee will tell him how many he still needs, but he will not give any clue as to the actual shot. The referee also arbitrates on any dispute.

The dartboard and the darts

It was much more difficult to write about dartboards 50 years ago than it is today. Soon after the 1939-45 War it was common to find regional boards in Britain. Today those boards are much less in evidence, and one board dominates the game: this is the 'clock' or 'treble' board.

The clock board

The distinctive feature of the clock board is its treble ring. This facilitates:

- higher scoring
- a greater variety of games to be played
- a greater variety of finishes in a straight scoring game.

The clock board and the growth of televised darts went hand in hand. A leg of 501-up, with a straight start (in other words, the player need not start on a double) can be completed in two or three minutes on a clock board, There is a quick build-up to the climax, when one player checks out on a double. Then the players are off again.

◀ *Conventional clock board*

You will probably recognise the numbering on the clock board on the previous page. The numbers are a subtle mixture, with the 20 flanked by two low numbers in 5 and 1. The 19 is flanked by 3 and 7; 18 by 1 and 4; and 17 by 2 and 3. Four odd numbers are clustered together at the bottom, namely 17, 3, 19 and 7; and three pairs of even numbers fall together – 18 and 4, 6 and 10, and 16 and 8. This 16-8 area is valuable for finishing a leg, as we will see later.

More and more people are hanging dartboards in their own homes, especially as they can be housed easily in a wood-grained wall cabinet. Many aspiring players have put up a board in a garage or an outhouse. But a word of warning here – the board must be hung at the right height and the throwing distance must be spot on (*see* figs 9 and 10), otherwise any practice becomes self-defeating.

Good players never practise using wrong measurements. By the same token, a professional will need to throw only three darts at a board to discover that it is slightly too high or too low.

Fig. 1 Dimensions of the clock board ▶

The dimensions of the clock board are shown in fig. 1. There is a difference between these and the dimensions of the BDO international dartboard. The double and treble beds on the BDO board are 11.1 mm ($\frac{7}{16}$ in) from the outside edges of the wire, whereas the traditional measurement is 9.5 mm ($\frac{3}{8}$ in). Thus the board used in televised BDO events gains $\frac{1}{16}$ in in four places across its diameter. It therefore has a playing area of 342.9 mm (13$\frac{1}{2}$ in) as against 336.5 mm (13$\frac{1}{4}$ in).

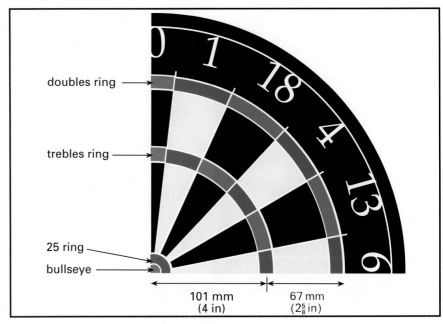

doubles ring

trebles ring

25 ring

bullseye

101 mm
(4 in)

67 mm
(2$\frac{5}{8}$ in)

Other boards

One unfortunate effect of the increased popularity of darts has been the decline of regional dartboards: all keen players hope to progress and that means they want to practise and compete on the clock board.

One of the most spectacular of the regional boards was the Grimsby Board which had 28 segments and no treble ring. The 28 was at the top, and the 20 was roughly at ten o'clock.

The Gloucestershire Board was almost twice as big as an orthodox board and had doubles and trebles about 12 mm ($\frac{1}{2}$ in) in width. Alas, like the Grimsby, the Gloucestershire is long dead.

Regional boards which still survive include the Yorkshire or Kent Board, the Lincoln or Medway Board, the Black Irish Board, Wide and Narrow Fives Boards, and the Log-End or Manchester Board.

◀ *Fig. 2 The Yorkshire or Kent board*

Fig. 3 The Lincoln ▶ or Medway board

The Yorkshire is a doubles board which does not have a treble ring but otherwise looks like the clock board. The Irish Board is an all-black version of the doubles board. The Lincoln Board is also all black but with a 381 mm (15 in) playing area as opposed to the 336.5 mm (13$\frac{1}{4}$ in) of the clock board.

Fives still survive in the East End of London and in parts of Suffolk. Figs 4 and 5 show the two different Fives Boards, one with wide doubles and trebles, the other with narrow doubles and trebles. Naturally, the games played on these boards are in units of five, for example 505-up instead of 501.

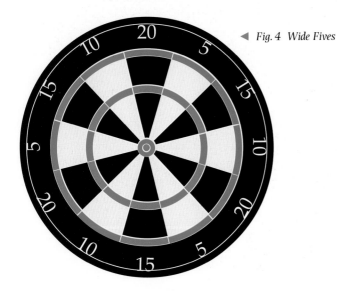

◀ *Fig. 4 Wide Fives*

Fig. 5 Narrow Fives ▶

The Log-End Board is the most unusual of the surviving regional boards. Fig. 6 shows that its numbering seems quite alien. The adherents of the board in Greater Manchester claim that it can be traced back to the battle of Agincourt in 1415. The English archers who won that famous victory practised on wooden targets lopped off the end of logs, and today the board is simply a log from an elm tree. The Log-End has a playing area of not more than 254 mm (10 in) across. The double ring is 3 mm ($\frac{1}{8}$ in) wide and the bullseye is less than 6 mm ($\frac{1}{4}$ in) across. It is difficult to play on.

The Champions' Choice is a board which is sometimes used for charity marathons. This board is similar to the clock board but the width of the double and treble ring is halved. Some players like to practise on the Champions' Choice Board. When they revert to an orthodox board, they hope the doubles and trebles will yawn out at them!

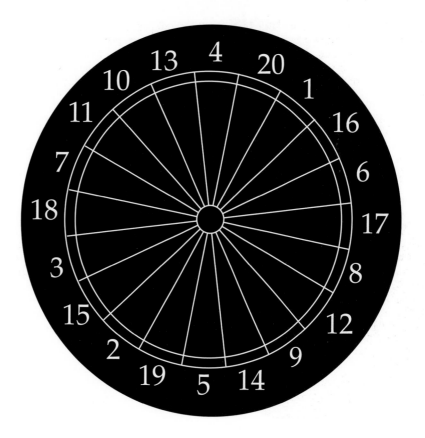

Fig. 6 Log-End ▶

9

Today's dartboards

Various materials have been used to make dartboards, among them cork and plasticine. Plasticine boards had to be rolled flat periodically and their other disadvantage was that they smelled. In 1930 a plasticine was discovered that did not smell and the result was the No Odour Company, based in East London. That company is with us today as Nodor.

Elm boards were regarded as the best for many years. Their disadvantage was that they had to be soaked regularly, otherwise they became hard and blunted the darts. This soaking caused the 'spider', that is the wire mesh that creates the scoring segments, to rust unless care was taken.

Boards made of compressed paper have long been popular, especially at the junior end of the market. But the bristle board became the most popular of all. This is made not of animal hair, as its name might suggest, but of vegetable matter. The Winmau company of Haverhill, Suffolk, imports sisal from Africa and cuts it up into 'biscuits' which are compressed into the dartboard shape. This is backed by chipboard and finished by screen-colouring and wiring.

In the 1970s players complained that dartboards seemed to comprise too much wire and too many staples. Darts which hit the wire and bounce out cannot be thrown again, and these 'bounce-outs' can be the difference between winning and losing. Manufacturers took notice and have reduced the area of wire; bounce-outs are not nearly as frequent as they were.

Today's darts

Darts used to be made of wood. The wooden, or French dart as it is often called, is still made in Belgium and France. But the wooden variety is rarely seen elsewhere now because, over the past 90 years, the dart has evolved rather like the motor car: the principles have remained the same but the finished product has changed a great deal in appearance.

A dart has four basic parts: a flight, a shaft, a barrel and a point (*see* fig. 7).

The point is invariably attached to the barrel. If the barrel is made of brass, the shaft and the flight will be together as one. If the barrel is made of tungsten, the shaft and flight probably will be detachable.

▼ *Fig. 7 The parts of a dart*

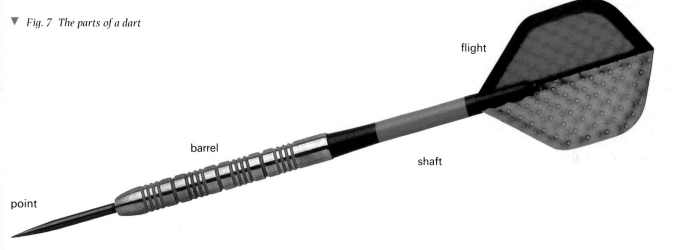

flight

barrel

shaft

point

The barrel is the key component. It can be of three basic shapes. There is a torpedo shape, which means the barrel is heavier at the front. There is a centre-weight shape, which means the barrel is thicker and heavier in the centre. Plus, there is the barrel that is the same thickness all the way down.

Barrels were usually made of brass 50 years ago. Today virtually all darts have barrels of tungsten or brass. By tungsten, we mean an alloy of nickel and tungsten. The advantage of tungsten is that it is 2.15 times denser than brass. Put another way, one cubic centimetre of tungsten will weigh 2.15 times the same volume of brass. This means tungsten can be made into a thin but still weighty dart.

Imagine that a player prefers a heavy dart, say 30–32 grams (1–1.1 oz) in weight. Made of brass, a dart of that weight would be very bulky. Many champions of old who used heavy darts would not attempt to hit three treble 20s because two fat brass darts in that bed would leave very little room to aim at. They had to risk losing their rhythm by switching to treble 19 or 18.

That is where tungstens come in. Even at 30 grams (1 oz) they are made thin enough to be handled with ease and to be grouped closely. They allow the player to hit 180 maximums, *if* he is skilful enough. They do not so easily block that key double 16 area if they go the wrong side of the wire when a player is trying to check out. But tungstens *do not* automatically fly straighter! Subconsciously, some players seem to think that they do.

Another advantage of tungsten not to be discounted is that they fit neatly into a smart leather wallet. This wallet is compact and can be produced from the breast pocket of a sport shirt with a flourish. Previously, brass darts, with their splendid feather flights, had to be kept in a plastic box which was quite bulky. Those boxes seem rather quaint today.

even

even

torpedo

centre

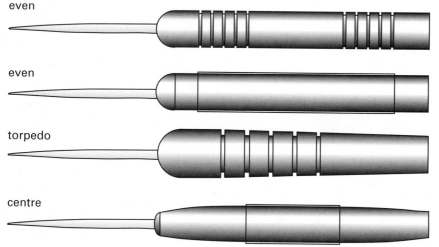

◀ *Fig. 8 Basic barrel shapes*

Shafts and flights

Tungsten darts come with a shaft which screws into the barrel. At the top of the shaft is an 'x'-shaped incision to take a flight which folds flat and unfolds. The shafts are made of various materials, including aluminium, glassfibre and cane. The flights are made of polyester or plastic.

Few darts players worry about the shape of their flights: they are more interested in the design, which is usually colourful and interesting.

The most basic brass dart carries a one-piece shaft and flight made of plastic.

Choosing your darts

The vast majority of county darts players throw tungsten darts. They are, after all, the really skilful players who can make use of the close groupings that tungstens allow. A pub player, for whom 45 is an average score, might prefer tungsten. Or he might decide that he is quite happy with his brass darts. He can loop these through the air, whereas he has to throw tungsten darts with a firmer, stronger action.

A disadvantage of tungsten is that it is more expensive than brass. A set of brass darts is relatively inexpensive: a tungsten set will cost nearly three times as much. If a pub player starts with brass darts and is happy with them, why spend the extra money? But a more ambitious player will want to switch to tungsten, and the sooner the better.

Today most tournament players throw a tungsten dart of 19 to 26 grams (0.67–0.9 oz) in weight. This applies equally to men and women, and to amateurs and professionals. One interesting development of the advent of tungstens is that players have moved towards lighter darts. Fewer and fewer players throw a dart weighing more than 28 grams (0.98 oz). This also means that more and more players are opting for straight-barrelled darts. It is impossible, for example, to have a torpedo-shaped tungsten dart of 21 grams (0.75 oz). At that weight, there isn't enough metal to create the torpedo shape!

It is a good idea for a player to experiment at the outset. Even if he thinks he has found his ideal dart at 28 grams, it is worthwhile experimenting with something both heavier and lighter. Sometimes a player will try for months, even years, to find the right dart for him. The answer may be to go to a manufacturer and to ask him to modify one of his existing range, or even to make a new dart to a definite specification.

Trial and error: this is often the only way to find the right set of darts. There are no fixed rules. Study the angle of your darts in the board. They should go in at a consistent angle, and that angle will be fairly flat when a tungsten thrower is aiming at treble 20.

It is important, psychologically as well as practically, to be perfectly happy with your darts. Then, if things go wrong, you know you have to blame the person who is throwing the darts and not the darts themselves.

The competition player will also want a back-up set of identical darts in case his first set gets lost or stolen. Also, he will without fail carry spare shafts and flights when he plays. Few things are more embarrassing for a player than to have to interrupt a match while he searches for a replacement shaft.

How high? How long?

The dimensions of the playing area are straightforward, The board must be hung with the centre of the bullseye 1.73 m (5 ft 8 in) above a point on the floor which is level with the area on which the player stands. The face of the board must be 2.37 m (7 ft 9¼ in) from the back of the 'oche'. The oche should be 610 mm (2 ft exactly) across and 38 mm (1½ in) high. *See* figs 9 and 10. (Obviously, there is no point hanging the board at 1.73 m if the player is standing on a worn stone floor which makes the height effectively a few centimetres more from the point at which the dart is thrown.)

Fig. 9 How high? How long? ▶
View from the side

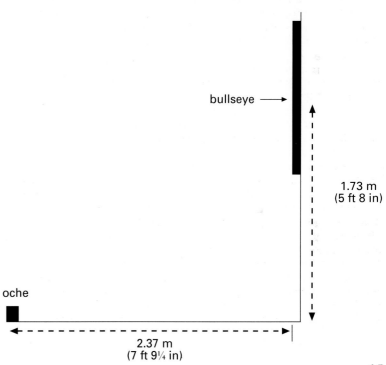

bullseye ⟶

1.73 m
(5 ft 8 in)

oche

2.37 m
(7 ft 9¼ in)

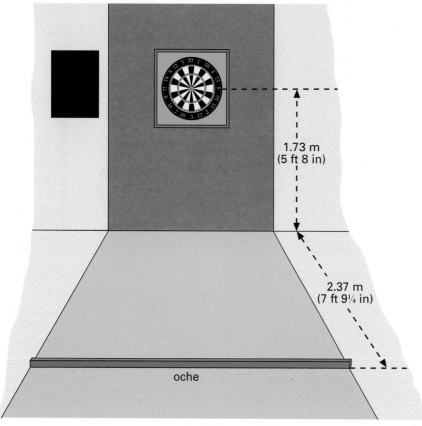

1.73 m
(5 ft 8 in)

2.37 m
(7 ft 9¼ in)

oche

The distance is taken from the *face* of the board, not from the wall behind it, and it is taken to the *back* of the oche. *Oche*, pronounced *okky*, is an old French word meaning to notch or to nick. Why modern darts should adopt such a word is obscure. It is arguable that the word is properly spelled *hockey*, and that it originates from the Hockey brewery in South-West England early in the twentieth century. Three Hockey crates were placed end to end to measure the 2.74 m (9 ft) that was then popular. Hence the phrase 'to toe the hockey'.

The oche is a strip of wood fastened to the floor to stop the player encroaching. Some pubs have a rubber mat with various lengths marked out in feet and inches. This mat does not always start from the face of the board and sometimes it becomes distorted with age. Some pubs have a brass strip screwed into the floor. However, for serious competition a raised oche is desirable.

◀ *Fig. 10 How high? How long? View from the oche*

If a player needs to stand wider than the 610 mm of the oche – and he might if his view of a double or treble bed is blocked – he must stay behind the imaginary line formed by the continuation of the oche.

The throwing distance of 2.37 m has become standardised. Fifty years ago distances ranged from 1.83 m (6 ft) to 2.74 m (9 ft). A compromise was reached at a meeting of the World Darts Federation in December 1977. Britain, the home of the game, used the imperial system of measurement and had been debating the merits of 7 ft 6 in and 8 ft. Naturally, the WDF worked with the metric system and defined those distances as 2.28 m and 2.44 m respectively. It decided on 2.37 m.

The throwing distance of 2.37 m ▶
has become standardised

Rules and formats – the straight scoring game

Basics

Of course, local leagues may adopt what rules suit them best. However, the following should be a useful guide.

● WDF and BDO rules stipulate that darts shall be a maximum of 50 g (1.76 oz) in weight and 30.5 cm (12 in) long, and must be thrown one at a time from a standing position unless the thrower is disabled.

● A dart scores only if its point is touching the board. Any dart which fails to stick in the board is invalid and may not be thrown again. If a dart is dropped and falls across the oche, it may still be thrown if the referee decides that it was not intentionally propelled towards the board.

● Darts count only after the score has been called by the referee (or, in a pub, written down by the 'chalker') and the darts have been retrieved by the thrower. This does not stop the player moving rapidly to the board to make safe his darts after he has thrown all three. But he may not interrupt his throw to secure a dart in the board.

● Before he throws, a player may ask the referee to check either his own or his opponent's score. The referee's decision is final.

● If a referee wrongly calls a game shot, the player may continue his throw to try to check out. Any darts withdrawn from the board by mistake should be put back.

● Any darts mistakenly thrown after a player has checked out do not count. It is impossible to bust a leg that has been successfully completed.

501 and 301

Most matches are of 501-up, straight start, finish on a double (or on the bull, which counts double 25). Certainly, this is the format for international matches and for nearly all major tournaments. In an international match, the format will be best-of-five-legs. In the bigger tournaments, 'sets' are used. In the Embassy World Professional Championship, the format is of sets, each set being best-of-five-legs. The first round is best-of-five-sets; the final is best-of-eleven-sets.

As far as format is concerned, the North American Open is an honourable exception. Players are confronted by a format of 301-up, start and finish on a double.

Who starts?

In large tournaments, who starts is decided by the toss of a coin or by the drawing of coloured balls from a bag. There is no second toss: if the match is all square with one leg remaining, the player whose turn it is starts the deciding leg.

Throwing first is a big advantage, rather like the tennis serve. Taking a leg 'against the darts', that is throwing second, is not easy against a competent player who may well start off by throwing 100 or more. Therefore, local leagues and smaller tournaments may have devised a different way to start. One option is 'middle for diddle' whereby the players throw at the bull and the nearer starts. Another way is for each player to throw six darts at the board, the higher scorer to start the match.

Equal darts

The idea that the toss of a coin is unfair is behind the periodic attempts to promote 'equal darts', or 'levelling out'. Many competitive matches are best-of-three-legs, 501-up. Therefore if the match goes to a third leg, the player throwing first has a huge advantage. A good player on form may well check out in 18 darts: to beat him, his opponent would have to check out in 15 darts. He would have to hit four successive 100s, then 101 in three darts, ending on a double – a tall order.

Equal darts or levelling out means that the player throwing second has a chance to draw or to win the leg. Thus, our first player hits an 18-dart 501. At this point player 2 has had only 15 darts. Under equal darts, he is now allowed to throw darts 16, 17 and 18 to see if he can tie or win the leg. If he hits a winning double with darts 16 and 17, he wins. If he does it with dart 18, the leg is tied and has to be replayed.

The main argument against equal darts is that it ruins the excitement of the tournament stage. On many occasions the crowd is going to be

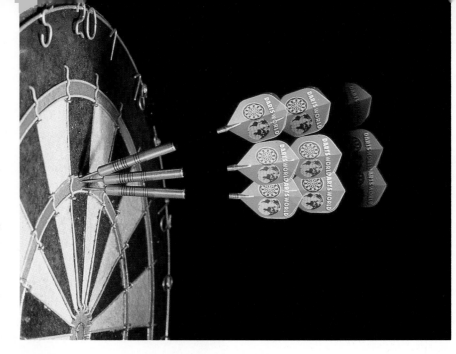

cheering a player's failure to level out, that being the end of the match, rather than the positive act of the winning player hitting his double. The counter argument is that equal darts gives everybody two phases of excitement at the end of a leg instead of one.

Bust rule

The BDO's version of the bust rule (Rule 11.03) is accepted everywhere: *If a player scores more than the number required, then that score shall not count and the player's score shall revert back to the score the player required prior to the opponent's last throw.*

This means that if a player wants 32 to finish and scores 16, 8 and 13, he must return to requiring 32 because he has scored too many (37). Do not merely count the 16 and the 8 to leave yourself double 4.

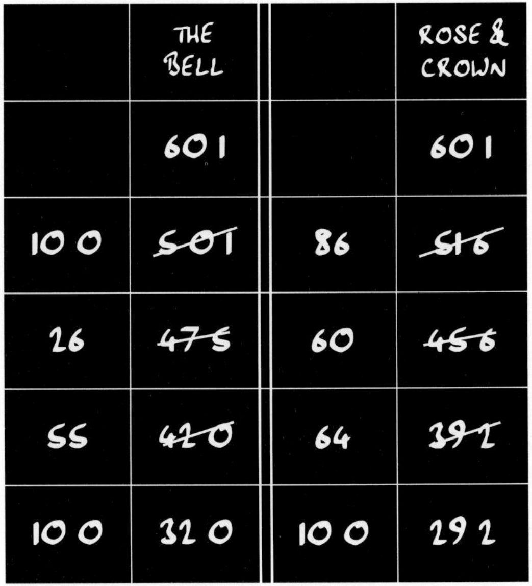

	THE BELL		ROSE & CROWN
	601		601
100	~~501~~	86	~~515~~
26	~~475~~	60	~~456~~
55	~~420~~	64	~~392~~
100	320	100	292

◀ *Fig. 11 Chalking a pub game*

Improve your play

Darts is different from other sports in one fundamental way. With soccer, tennis, hockey and most other ball games, save perhaps golf, what your opponent does is paramount. You react to what he does. With darts, you are playing against the board.

It is a great help to thrust your opponent and the surroundings out of your mind as far as possible. All that matters is how well you throw. If you could complete every 501 leg in the minimum of nine darts, you would never lose a leg; ten, 11, 12, or 13 darts for every leg and you would never lose a match; 14 or 15 darts and you would lose very rarely; 15 to 20 darts and you would win some and lose some; more than 20 darts every leg and you would not beat an international player.

Remember this and adopt a positive approach to playing.

ally it is sporting. So don't rattle loose change or click your darts while your opponent is throwing. If you smoke, be sensitive to the comfort and concentration of the opponent. If you are sporting, if you look down on any skulduggery, it will give you confidence.

Preparation and planning

For most players darts is fun. They can enjoy themselves in a pleasant atmosphere and not take it too badly if they have lost. But anybody who is determined to win a day long darts open, or a single match, should approach that task in the same way that a soccer player might approach a cup tie. This is no exaggeration. The darts player should:

● try to be at the top of his physical and mental form
● be organised and impeccably turned out. This gives him a psychological advantage.
● assume that he is going to progress to the end of an event that may last eight hours or more. He should know in advance how often he will need to play, and how he can best use his breaks between rounds.
● be sporting to a fault. Competitive darts can be a niggling affair, but usu-

Practice

Darts players are made, they are not born. Top players win championships because they have natural talent but also because they practise for up to eight hours a day.

Most top players do not practise by playing a full leg of 501. They will start at, say, 301 and work their way down from there. If they are very confident they may aim to leave themselves 170 because this is the highest check-out possible and often carries a substantial cash prize in tournaments if achieved. But whatever method they choose, they will practise for hours on end and against a first class opponent. To practise on your own is difficult: it becomes boring and disorganised.

Practise those doubles!

Goals are vital to soccer, catches are vital to cricket, and doubles are vital to darts. Practising doubles is essential to players of all levels.

Again, it is better to practise against an opponent than to practise solo. Start 1, 2, 3 rather than moving clockwise round the board.

A good doubles game is for each player to draw out of a hat three numbers between 1 and 20 (or you can do something similar with playing cards). Keep your three numbers secret. You have to hit your opponent's doubles before he hits yours, even though you don't know what his doubles are. Some bluffing adds to the fun. If you have double 9, throw a couple of darts at it, but make sure you miss. If you hit your own double, scrub it off your list. When the opponent hits your number, toss your piece of paper on to the table. When your three numbers are hit, you have lost.

Stance

Formal technique is not important in darts. The end product is the only thing that matters. Each individual achieves that end product in his own way.

A player needs to achieve two things from his stance: perfect balance and perfect stillness. He needs to eliminate the slightest body movement when he throws because that wobble will translate itself to his aim.

There are three basic stances.

● **Straight on.** Tom Barrett, the best player in the world in the mid-1960s, used to maintain a beautiful stance. He stood upright, as still as a statue, with his feet close together and his toes pointing through the oche at right angles to and towards the board. When he threw, his trunk did not move.

● **Sideways.** The player plants his feet parallel to the oche with his shoulder pointing towards the board. This enables him to put more weight on his leading foot (his right foot if he is right-handed and vice versa) and to lean forwards when he throws.

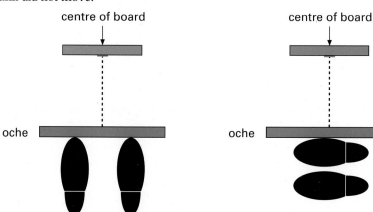

▲ *Fig. 12 Straight on stance*

▲ *Fig. 13 Sideways stance*

● **Best foot forward.** The player places his leading foot against the oche at about 45° to it. His back foot is half off the floor when he throws, with only the ball of the foot anchored.

Most players regard the straight-on stance as rather outdated. A relaxed, best-foot-forward stance is probably the ideal to aim at for most players. Don't wobble when you throw, and take up an identical stance every time you play.

Pick your spot on the oche very carefully. There is no point practising for hours from one point on the oche, then moving a couple of inches to the left when you come to play.

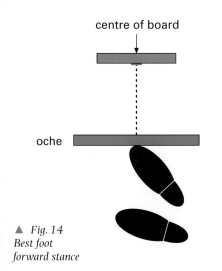

▲ *Fig. 14*
Best foot
forward stance

Grip

It is advisable to carry a piece of chalk in your pocket so that from time to time you can dry the damp ends of your fingers.

Your grip should be such that the dart flies out of your hand cleanly. You will probably grip the dart between the thumb and first finger, with the middle finger providing support. Grip the dart in exactly the same way and at exactly the same point on the barrel each time. Try taking your fingers away and resting the dart only on the thumb. The angle at which the dart rests will enable you to gauge precisely where you are holding the dart.

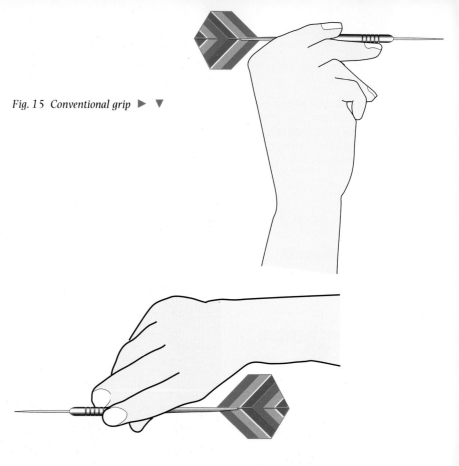

Fig. 15 Conventional grip ▶ ▼

The throw

Watch the most successful players and you will soon notice that they will throw their darts like a machine. Most of their movement will be from the elbow joint down. They will not push the dart from the shoulder. They will not raise their throwing hand a few inches and toss the dart in a loop. Four fundamental rules to remember are:

● **throw, don't lob;** unless, of course, your path to a particular bed is blocked and you are trying to loop a dart in
● **take your time:** modern darts can be highly organised and run to a tight schedule; slow throwing has been discouraged of late, but players should refuse to be rushed

Throw, don't lob ▶

- **release the dart at the same point each time:** if your delivery point varies, you will find it very hard to be consistent; if your delivery is smooth, you will develop a natural delivery point; if you are nervous and staccato in your movements, your chances are drastically reduced in achieving consistency
- **follow through:** imagine trying to kick a ball first with a stabbing motion then with a sweeping follow through; there is no doubt which is likely to be the more accurate – so it is with darts.

▲ *Take your time*

Follow through ▶

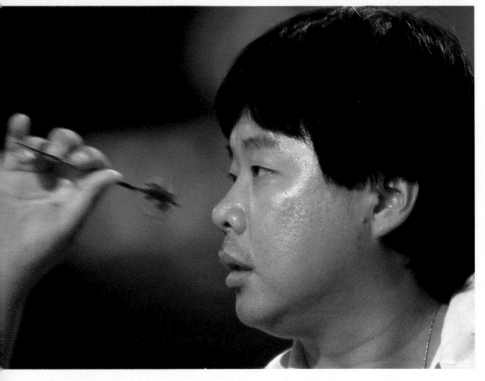

Don't waste a dart

To beat a professional player, with all his experience, is extremely difficult. To do so it is essential to make every dart count. This is another essential rule. **Never waste a dart.** It is surprising how many players do waste their darts. There are three common examples of this.

● Some players throw their very first dart, or even their first three darts, as a warming-up exercise, as a 'loosener'.

● If the first two darts have scored badly, some players throw or flick the third one at the board in disgust. How foolish. If you are frustrated, step back from the oche for a moment, take a breath, then aim again.

● When attempting an out shot, especially on an odd number double, there is a temptation to use the first dart as a marker, to 'feel the lie of the land'. Don't: it seldom helps. If you are on double 5 and you are frightened of splitting it, better to go 2, double 4 right away.

Finishing

Of course, a beginner often wastes a dart because he makes a wrong decision as he scores down to a finishing double. He may not ask anybody's advice. The referee will tell him that he needs 82; he will not tell him 'which way to go', i.e. how to score the 82. Even with numbers of 40 and under, the player will be told that he needs, say, 36 and not double 18.

Back to 82. Our novice has a number of choices here. He might go treble 18, double 14. But if he hits single 18 instead of the treble, he is left with 64, and that means he has still to hit a treble and a double to check out. Or he has to go 14, bull, but he is not yet confident on the bull. Treble 14, double 20 used to be the accepted way of achieving 82. But that has the same disadvantage: miss and you have two difficult shots left.

That is why an experienced player would probably choose to go bull double 16. He reasons that if he misses the bull he'll probably hit the 25-ring instead.

That leaves him 57, a good two-dart shot of single 17, double 20.

Don't be frightened of carrying around with you a list of out shots until you become more familiar with them. Don't take the easy way out and automatically go for treble 20 whenever an out shot of more than 100 is left. On, say, 137 it is perhaps natural to hope to hit treble 20, and then 'sort out' the remaining 77. But it would be more sensible to develop a liking for treble 19, treble 16, double 16. That way, you are aiming at the same bed for your last two darts; and checking out with two darts in the 16 bed is a bit special!

Three basic rules apply to finishing:

● **Finish simply.** Top players have become more and more fond of bull finishes. One reason is that when they play exhibitions, the spectators like to see these: the habit has stuck in tournament play. There is a good deal of logic in bull finishes because a top player can calculate that even if he misses the bull,

he may still hit 25. Each player must make his own decision here. If you are skilled at hitting the bull, practise bull finishes – they are great when they come off. If you are less confident, go for the simple finishes.

● **Tailor your outs to the game.** We have said that what your opponent does is irrelevant. Forget him. The one exception to this is when, say, he is stuck back at 221 and you are nearly home, needing 71 in two darts. You can go treble 13, double 16, but you would rather go for double top (i.e. double 20). You have not missed it all day. Therefore, decide that you are going to come back to the board and simply reduce the 71 to 40 in two darts. OK, you have broken another golden rule: you have deliberately wasted a dart. But you have tailored your out shot to the game. Similarly, if you have plenty in hand and you are left needing a difficult number, do not be afraid to bust.

- **Work down to 32.** The advantages are obvious: 32 requires double 16; score single 16 and you can move next door to double 8. You can split double 8, double 4 and double 2 without having to waste a dart on any single number. Also, should you hit single 8 instead of double 16, you can move on to double 12.

- **Or work down to 40.** There are plenty of players who swear by double top. Double 20 splits to double 10, a favourite double for many, and again to double 5. But, of course, the great appeal of double 20 is that many players find it the easiest to hit. The game is, after all, usually geared to hitting the 20 bed. Therefore you have to make a choice in the lower reaches. With 53 left, it is natural to go 13, double 20. With 52 left, you can either go 12, double 20, or 20, double 16. And so on down to 41. Below 41, the choice between double 20 and double 16 no longer exists.

Recommended finishes

180	4 darts	**167**	T20 T19 bull	**154**	T18 T20 D20
179	4 darts	**166**	4 darts	**153**	T20 T19 D18
178	4 darts	**165**	4 darts	**152**	T20 T20 D16
177	4 darts	**164**	T20 T18 bull	**151**	T17 T20 D20
176	4 darts	**163**	4 darts	**150**	T20 T18 D18
175	4 darts	**162**	4 darts	**149**	T20 T19 D16
174	4 darts	**161**	T20 T17 bull	**148**	T20 T20 D14 *or* T20 T16 D20
173	4 darts	**160**	T20 T20 D20	**147**	T20 T17 D18
172	4 darts	**159**	4 darts	**146**	T20 T18 D16
171	4 darts	**158**	T20 T20 D19	**145**	T20 T15 D20
170	T20 T20 bull	**157**	T19 T20 D20	**144**	T20 T20 D12
169	4 darts	**156**	T20 T20 D18	**143**	T20 T17 D16
168	4 darts	**155**	T20 T19 D19	**142**	T20 T14 D20

141	T20 T19 D12	127	T20 T17 D8	113	T20 13 D20
140	T20 T20 D10 *or* T20 T16 D16	126	T19 T11 D18 *or* T20 T18 D6	112	T20 12 D20
139	T20 T13 D20	125	T20 T11 D16 *or* T20 T19 D4	111	T20 19 D16 *or* T17 20 D20
138	T20 T18 D12	124	T20 T16 D8	110	T20 18 D16
137	T19 T16 D16 *or* T20 T15 D16	123	T20 T13 D12	109	T20 17 D16
136	T20 T20 D8	122	T18 D18 D16	108	T20 16 D16
135	T20 T15 D15	121	T19 T16 D8	107	T19 10 D20 *or* T19 18 D16
134	T20 T14 D16	120	T20 20 D20	106	T20 10 D18 *or* T20 14 D16
133	T20 T19 D8	119	T20 19 D20 *or* T19 T10 D16	105	T20 13 D16
132	T20 T16 D12	118	T20 18 D20	104	T20 12 D16 *or* T18 18 D16
131	T20 T13 D16	117	T20 17 D20 *or* T19 20 D20	103	T17 20 D16
130	T20 T18 D8	116	T20 20 D18	102	T20 10 D16
129	T20 T11 D18	115	T20 15 D20	101	T17 10 D20 *or* T17 18 D16
128	T20 T20 D4	114	T20 18 D18 *or* T20 14 D20	100	T20 D20

99	T19 10 D16	**85**	T15 D20	**71**	T13 D16
98	T20 D19	**84**	T20 D12	**70**	T10 D20
97	T19 D20	**83**	T17 D16	**69**	T11 D18
96	T20 D18	**82**	Bull D16	**68**	T20 D4
95	T19 D19	**81**	T19 D12	**67**	T17 D8
94	T18 D20	**80**	T20 D10 *or* T16 D16	**66**	T18 D6 *or* T10 D18
93	T19 D18	**79**	T13 D20	**65**	T19 D4
92	T20 D16	**78**	T18 D12	**64**	T16 D8
91	T17 D20	**77**	T15 D16	**63**	T17 D6 *or* T13 D12
90	T18 D18	**76**	T20 D8	**62**	T14 D10
89	T19 D16	**75**	T13 D18	**61**	T15 D8
88	T16 D20	**74**	T14 D16	**60**	20 D20
87	T17 D18	**73**	T19 D8	**59**	19 D20
86	T18 D16	**72**	T16 D12	**58**	18 D20

57	17 D20	43	11 D16	29	13 D8	15	7 D4
56	16 D20	42	10 D16	28	D14	14	D7
55	15 D20	41	9 D16	27	11 D8	13	5 D4
54	14 D20	40	D20	26	D13	12	D6
53	13 D20	39	7 D16	25	9 D8	11	3 D4
52	20 D16	38	D19	24	D12	10	D5
51	19 D16	37	5 D16	23	7 D8	9	1 D4
50	18 D16	36	D18	22	D11	8	D4
49	17 D16	35	3 D16	21	5 D8	7	3 D2
48	16 D16	34	D17	20	D10	6	D3
47	15 D16	33	1 D16	19	3 D8	5	1 D2
46	14 D16	32	D16	18	D9	4	D2
45	13 D16	31	15 D8	17	1 D8	3	1 D1
44	12 D16	30	D15	16	D8	2	D1
						1	score has bust

Games to play

There are many other enjoyable forms of darts. Some of the most popular are listed below. The rules often vary from area to area.

MICKEY MOUSE

JOHN			ANDY	
60 ~~60~~ ✝✝✝	20		✝✝✝	
┃┃┃	19		✝✝✝	38
┃┃┃	18		✝┃┃	
┃┃┃	17		┃┃┃	
┃┃┃	16		┃┃┃	
┃┃┃	15		┃┃┃	
┃┃┃	14		┃┃┃	
┃┃┃	13		┃┃┃	
┃┃✝	12		┃┃┃	
┃✝✝	11		✝┃┃	
┃┃┃	BULL		┃┃┃	

◀ *Fig. 16 Mickey Mouse*

Mickey Mouse

An excellent game which goes under numerous names. (In many areas it is called 'Tactics'.) To play, chalk up a scoreboard as in fig. 16. The bull can stand for bullseye, or it can stand for 25 (the outer bull). In this second instance, if you hit a bull it counts as two 25s.

Both players or teams have three marks against each number. To score on any number you have to hit three of it (one treble, a double and a single or three singles). Then, and only then, can you start scoring on that number. But if your opponent hits three of a number before you do, all you can do is to eliminate it. For instance, if he is scoring on 20 he continues until you hit three of them.

It is not difficult to see why the game is called Tactics. Your opponent is scoring on 19s, you are scoring on 11s and 14s (the only two of these numbers which are together on the board). Who will be the first to break ranks and eliminate the other's numbers, or suddenly switch the attack to 18s, or to the bull?

When a player has a sufficient lead in points scored, he will try to eliminate his opponent's remaining options. Obviously, there comes a point when one player has lost – i.e he is behind and he cannot score any more.

Shanghai

Set off round the board on the 1, 2 and 3 segments, intending to go as far as 9. Take it in turns to aim three darts at single 1, double 1 and treble 1. Then move on to 2, and so on. Score only on your target number; that is, double 1, plus single 1, plus 18 scores 3 points. At any time, Shanghai – that is, one dart in the single, one in the double, and one in the treble – wins the game. But the round must be completed, and if two players end with Shanghai on, say, 5, the player with the greater number of points wins.

It is customary to eliminate anybody who misses completely when aiming for 3, 5 or 7. Remember to aim for a specific target with every dart, rather than going for the general area of the number and trusting to luck.

37

Halve-it

For this game, write down a series of targets. If you hit them, you score what you score. If you miss with all three darts, you halve your total score, and if you miss three times on the trot you are eliminated.

Let us take a possible sequence: 11, 12, double, 13, 14, 'outer ring', 15, 16, treble, 17, 18, 'inner ring', 19, 20, bull or 25 ring. The outer ring means all three darts must land in the area between the double and the treble bands; the inner ring means all three darts must land in the area between the treble band and the 25 ring. Therefore, if you hit a double or a treble while throwing for the outer ring or the inner ring, you halve your total score. If you hit a treble or the bull or 25 going for the inner ring, you also have to halve it. It is amazing how many players fail to get three darts in the outer ring.

Noughts and crosses

As in the more traditional form of noughts and crosses, chalk nine spaces. Write a target into each space, the degree of difficulty depending on the standard of the players. The target in the centre square should be the most difficult of all. The first player to hit a line of three targets wins.

English cricket

One player bats and scores runs for every point he scores over, say, 60 – thus, 62 scores 2 runs. The other player bowls and takes one wicket for hitting the 25 ring and two wickets for hitting the bull. The batsman inadvertently hits his own wicket if he hits the 25 ring or bull.

BDO playing rules

All darts events in Great Britain that are organised under the exclusive supervision of the British Darts Organisation Ltd., or its subsidiaries, shall be played under the BDO Playing Rules.

The BDO Playing Rules are divided into two distinctly separate groups: General Playing Rules – numbered 1 to 15 inclusive; Tournament Playing Rules – numbered 16 to 32 inclusive.

All the Rules have been numbered consecutively to avoid any confusion between the numbers used in each group.

Some of the Rules have several Clauses which are also numbered consecutively relative to the Rule Heading, so that each Clause can be easily identified.

Definitions

Various 'terms' have been used within the Rules for simplification; these are defined below for reference.

- 'BDO' – shall mean the British Darts Organisation Limited, or any of its subsidiaries.
- 'Organisers' – shall mean the British Darts Organisation Ltd., its Directors, or persons appointed by the British Darts Organisation Ltd., to carry out its functions in relation to a darts event.

- 'Player' – shall mean singular and plural, and shall include juniors, youths, men, women, and teams.
- 'Referee' – shall mean the person appointed to take charge of matchplay at a MatchBoard, or on stage, and shall include those persons sometimes referred to as 'callers', or 'checkers'.
- 'Marker' – shall mean the person appointed to mark scores down on score sheets, or a score board, at a MatchBoard, or on stage, and shall include those persons sometimes referred to as 'scorers'.
- 'Scores recorder' – shall mean the person appointed to record all scores and enter all relevant matchplay details on official BDO Result Sheets, or Record Cards.
- 'Dartboard indicator operator' – shall mean the person appointed to operate the electrical dartboard indicator equipment located on the stage, which indicates to the audience which segments the players darts have landed in.

General playing rules

1.00 Players shall provide their own darts, which shall not exceed an overall maximum length of 30.5 cm, (12 in) nor weigh more than 50 g. Each dart shall consist of a needle shaped point, which shall be fixed to a barrel. At the rear of the barrel shall be an attached flighted stem, which may consist of up to three separate pieces, i.e. a flight, a flight securing device, and a stem.

2.00 The BDO reserves the right to seed players, in certain events, when it is deemed necessary.

3.00 All players, and teams shall play within the BDO Playing Rules, and, where necessary, any supplementary Rules laid down in an entry form, or programme.

4.00 All players, and teams, shall play under the supervision and direction of BDO appointed Organisers, and Officials, in all darts events organised under the jurisdiction of the BDO.

5.00 All trophies awarded to a player shall be retained, unless they are of a challenge, or perpetual type, which shall be returned to the BDO on request.

6.00 Any player failing to comply with any of the BDO Playing Rules during an event shall be liable to disqualification from that event.

7.00 The interpretation of the BDO Playing Rules in relation to a darts event shall be determined by the BDO appointed Organisers, whose decision shall be final and binding.

8.00 Information concerning such interpretations shall be forwarded to the BDO Board of Directors for consideration and possible inclusion in a revised version of the BDO Playing Rules.

9.00 Any matter not expressly covered by the BDO Playing Rules shall be determined by the Board of Directors, whose decisions shall be final and binding.

10.00 Throw

10.01 A player shall throw darts from a standing position, excepting only in those circumstances when a physical disability, or physical injury requires a player to adopt a non-standing position, i.e. a wheelchair, or a similar form of support.

10.02 All darts must be deliberately thrown, one at a time, by, and from, the player's hand.

10.03 A throw shall consist of a maximum of 'three' darts, unless a leg, set, or match is completed in less than 'three' darts.

10.04 If a player 'touches' any dart, which is in the dartboard, during a throw, then that throw shall be deemed to have been completed.

10.05 Any dart bouncing off, or falling out of, the dartboard, does not count, and shall not be re-thrown.

11.00 Starting and finishing

11.01 In all darts events each leg shall be played with a straight start, and the finish must be on a 'double', unless stated otherwise in the playing format of a particular event.

11.02 The 'Bull' shall count as '50', and if '50' is required to complete a leg, set, or match, then the 'Bull' shall count as 'Double 25'.

11.03 The 'Bust' rule shall apply, i.e. if a player scores more than the number required then that score shall not count, and the player's score shall revert back to the score the player required prior to the opponent's last throw.

11.04 A 'Game Shot' called by a referee is valid, only if the darts thrown achieve the required finish, and remain in the dartboard until retrieved by the player at the time that 'Game Shot' is called.

11.05 If a 'Game Shot' called by a referee is declared invalid, then the player shall have the right to continue the throw, which is in progress, in an attempt to achieve the required finish.

11.06 If as a result of the error declared in Clause 11.05 the player has retrieved a dart, or darts, then the referee shall replace the dart, or darts, in as near as is practicable the same position, or positions, and then invite the player to complete that throw.

11.07 The BDO does not recognise the principle of 'equal darts', a player who finishes by obtaining the points required in accordance with the BDO Playing Rules wins that leg, set, or match, whichever is applicable.

The only exception to this Clause is in those events when an equal number of darts are allocated to players in a specific playing format.

11.08 Any darts mistakenly thrown by a player after scoring the required 'double' shall not be counted, as the respective leg, set, or match is concluded by the dart scoring the required 'double'.

12.00 Scoring

12.01 A dart shall only score if the point remains in, or touches the face of the dartboard, within the outer double wire, and having been 'called', shall be retrieved from the dartboard by the player.

12.02 The score is counted from the side of the segment wire in which the point of the dart enters and remains in, or touching, the face of the dartboard.

12.03 Darts shall be retrieved from the dartboard by the thrower but only after the score has been 'called' by the referee, and recorded by the marker.

12.04 A protest about the score attained, or called, after the retrieval of the dart, or darts, may not be upheld.

12.05 All scores, and subtractions made, should be checked by the referee, the marker, and the players after each throw, and where practicable, before the next player's throw commences.

12.06 All requests by a player to check scores recorded, or subtractions made, must be made before that player's next throw.

12.07 The actual score required by a player, must be shown on the score sheet, clearly visible, at eye level, in front of the players and the referee.

12.08 No indication of the required 'double' shall be given by the marker, or the referee, i.e. '32' required and NOT 'Double 16'.

12.09 The first player to reduce the score required to exactly zero, by obtaining the required 'double', is the winner of that leg, set, or match, whichever is applicable.

12.10 The referee shall act as an umpire in all matters pertaining to the BDO Playing Rules when conducting a darts match, and shall, if it is necessary, consult with scorers, and other officials, before announcing any decisions during the course of matchplay.

12.11 For an example of Setting out a Score Sheet, or Scoreboard, contact the B: O.

13.00 Dartboards

13.01 All dartboards shall be of the 'Bristle' type.

13.02 All dartboards shall be of the '1–20' Clock pattern.

13.03 The inner narrow band shall score 'Treble' the segment number.

13.04 The outer narrow band shall score 'Double' the segment number.

13.05 The outer centre ring shall score '25'.

13.06 The inner centre ring shall score '50', and shall be called the 'Bull'.

13.07 All the wires forming the segments; doubles; trebles; inner and outer centre rings, which together form the 'Spider' shall be affixed to the face of the dartboard in such a manner that they lie flat on the face of the dartboard.

13.08 The dartboard shall be fixed in such a manner that the perpendicular height from the floor to the centre of the 'Bull', at the same level as the Oche, shall measure 1.73 m (5 ft 8 in). *See* diagram on page 15.

13.09 The dartboard shall be fixed such that the '20' segment is coloured 'black', and is at the top of the dartboard.

13.10 The BDO INTERNATIONAL DARTBOARD shall be used in all BDO darts events. For more details, contact the BDO.

13.11 A player, or team captain, shall have the right to request that a dartboard be changed, or moved, during the course of a match, always providing that the opposing player, or team captain, concurs with the request. Such change, or move, shall only be made before the start of, or after the completion of a leg.

13.12 Adjustments to the position of, or changing of, a dartboard, shall only be carried out by a BDO appointed match official.

14.00 Lighting

14.01 In tournament play all 'floor' dartboards shall be adequately lit by a suitably positioned light fitting at each dartboard, i.e. 100 Watt minimum intensity.

14.02 Dartboards used in 'stage finals' shall be adequately lit by suitably positioned light fittings, i.e. two 100 Watt minimum intensity fittings.

14.03 All light fittings must be fitted with screens to divert all light away from the player's eyes when standing at the Oche.

14.04 In 'stage finals' the general level of illumination can be augmented by the use of 'floods' and 'spotlights', but extreme care is needed to prevent the introduction of unwanted 'shadows' on the dartboard during matchplay.

15.00 Oches

15.01 A raised Oche, 38 mm high and 610 mm long, (1.5 in high and 24 in long), must be placed in position at the minimum throwing distance and shall measure from the back of the raised Oche 2.37 m (7 ft 9.25 in) along the floor to a plumb line at the face of the dartboard.

15.02 The diagonal distance from the Centre Bull to the back of the raised Oche at floor level shall measure 2.93 m (9 ft 7.5 in).

15.03 In those circumstances where the Oche is set down on a raised Playing Area, then the raised Playing Area must be constructed such that it is centrally placed in relation to the dartboard; the minimum width at the Oche shall not be less than 1525 mm (5 ft 0 in); and the minimum depth of the standing area to the rear of the Oche shall be not less than 1200 mm (4 ft 0 in).

15.04 During matchplay no player shall tread on any part of the raised Oche, nor shall the player deliver any dart with his feet in any position other than behind the toe edge of the raised Oche.

15.05 A player wishing to throw a dart, or darts, from a point on either side of the raised Oche must keep his feet behind an imaginary straight line extending on either side of the raised Oche.

15.06 Any player in breach of Clause 15.04, or 15.05, shall first be warned by the referee in the presence of the Player's Captain, or Team Manager. Any dart subsequently delivered in breach of these Clauses shall not score, and shall be declared invalid by the referee.

15.07 A player, or team captain, shall have the right to request that the Oche dimensions be checked, and adjusted if necessary, always providing that the opposing player, or team captain, concurs with the request.

Such request must be made before the start of, or after the completion of a Leg.

The match official shall, at his discretion, convey the request to the Stage Manager, or Floor Controller, so that a check, and adjustment if necessary, can be effected.

Such check, and any adjustment, shall only be made before the start of, or after the completion of a leg.

15.08 Adjustments to, and the checking of, Oche dimensions shall only be carried out by a BDO appointed match official.

15.09 Oche dimensions – contact the BDO.

16.00 Tournament and championship playing rules

16.01 Unless stated otherwise all BDO Tournaments, and Championships, shall be run on a 'Knock-Out' basis.

16.02 Special events, or multiple team Play-offs, may involve a 'Round-Robin' basis, i.e. each player, or team, plays every other player, or team in that event.

16.03 The BDO, or its appointed Organisers, reserve the right to cancel, or change, all dates, venues, and scheduled darts events, without prior notice.

16.04 Decisions on all matters pertaining to the BDO Playing Rules in any BDO Tournament, or Championship, shall be made by the appointed Organisers, whose decisions shall be final and binding.

16.05 In County Play-offs, where the number of entries for that County have been allocated into sections to be played off at different dates, times, and playing venues, it is acceptable for players to be re-allocated on request.

Such re-allocation, however, is subject to being sanctioned in writing, by the appointed Organisers, prior to the date of the original allocation with a copy of the sanction being sent to the BDO Office for future reference in the instance of any enquiry.

16.06 All tournament players shall play within the BDO Playing Rules, and where necessary, any supplementary Rules laid down in a darts event entry form, or programme.

16.07 Any player, or team, found guilty of deliberately losing a leg, set, or match, shall be disqualified from any further participation in that particular BDO darts event, that player, or team, shall also be barred from entering any other BDO darts event until such time as laid down by the Board of Directors.

16.08 No player, nor a team, having been knocked out of a 'Knock-Out Tournament' shall play again in that Tournament, either as a substitute player, or team or in his, or their own right, excepting in those circumstances when a breach of the BDO Playing Rules has occurred which materially affected the losing player, or team, such breach not having been occasioned by the losing player, or team. The BDO appointed Organisers may, at their own discretion, reinstate the player, or team, in the Tournament, either in substitution for, or in addition to the winning player, or team.

This Clause shall be constructed as embracing any number of players up to, and including, a complete team.

16.09 If a player, or team representative, is not present at the official presentation ceremonies to receive trophies, prizes, or prize monies, without the BDO appointed Organiser's, or the Sponsor's prior permission, then that player, or team representative, shall forfeit the right to receive any such trophies, prizes, or prize monies that may be due.

16.10 Any player, or team, not fulfilling the playing commitments of a Tournament by failing to complete all scheduled matches, including Grand Finals, shall forfeit the right to receive any trophies, prizes, or prize monies that may be due in relation to that respective Tournament.

16.11 If any additional expenses are incurred due to a default by a player, or team then that player, or team shall be liable for those additional expenses.

16.12 In the instance of a player, or team being involved in, or causing, actions which are considered to have brought the Sport of Darts into disrepute, then that player, or team shall be liable to Disciplinary Proceedings being taken against the player, or team, which could mean the imposition of fines, suspensions, or other penalties.

See the BDO Code of Practice No III in the BDO Authorised Handbook.

17.00 Entry

17.01 Admission fees into tournament venues are not refundable.

17.02 Entry fees into tournaments are not refundable, except on those occasions deemed appropriate by the Board of Directors.

17.03 All entries are to be made on official BDO entry forms, which must be accurately completed and returned, together with the appropriate entry fees, before, or on the specified closing date.

17.04 Any entry form found to be inaccurately completed, or not submitted strictly in accordance with the requirements laid down on the entry form, may not be accepted by the Organisers, or the entry disqualified before, during, or after the event depending upon when the inaccuracy is discovered.

17.05 The first named player, or representative, on a team entry form shall assume the responsibility of notifying the second, or other named players, of the receipt of, and the contents of all communications in connection with the darts event received by him from the BDO appointed Organisers.

17.06 The receipt of an entry form will only be acknowledged if a self addressed envelope is enclosed with the entry form, together with sufficient postage to cover the return of the receipt.

17.07 Only the players named on an entry form as the competing individual, or team, shall be eligible to play in the respective darts event.

17.08 No player, or team, shall enter more than once in any respective darts event.

17.09 No player shall play in more than one team in any respective darts event.

17.10 All players participating in a Singles, or Pairs darts event must play under their own name.

17.11 Unless stated otherwise all entry fees shall be used exclusively in defraying tournament expenses; to further the promotion of the Sport of Darts; or to support a specific charity.

17.12 The completion of an entry form by a player, or team, for a BDO darts event, and the acceptance of that entry form by the BDO, shall be deemed as an acceptance by that player, or team, of the BDO Playing Rules in relation to that event.

17.13 The BDO appointed Organisers reserve the right to refuse, or cancel, any entrant, at any stage prior to, during, or after a darts event, without assigning a reason for so doing, and their decision shall be final and binding in all matters relating to that event.

17.14 Any entrant into a BDO Members-Only darts event is always subject to the player complying with the BDO Eligibility Rule.

18.00 Registration

18.01 All tournament players shall register at each darts event at scheduled times, which are predetermined by the BDO appointed Organisers.

18.02 Any tournament player failing to register by the notified time shall be eliminated from that respective tournament, in which instance no entry fee shall be refundable.

18.03 No player shall be allowed to register more than once in any respective darts event in any one Playing Season.

18.04 Any player, or team, that is not in attendance when called upon to play at the nominated time shall forfeit that leg, set, or match, whichever is applicable; in such instances no entry fee shall be refundable.

18.05 Only THREE minutes shall be allowed from the time of calling over the public address system for the player, or team, to reach the Control Desk, or the Assigned MatchBoard, whichever requirement is being called for.

18.06 The BDO appointed Organisers reserve the right to alter scheduled times and the Playing Format of a darts event whenever it is deemed necessary.

18.07 Any player, or team, has the right to be advised the time of the next match that the player, or team is scheduled to play.

19.00 Draw

19.01 There will be only ONE draw for opponents which shall be conducted prior to the darts event, the bracket system being adopted.

19.02 The BDO appointed Organisers shall arrange preliminary matches so as to eliminate all 'Byes' from the first round proper of the darts event.

19.03 Draw Charts must be displayed, where possible, at the Control Desk, in the event programme, at the MatchBoard, or at a convenient point in the venue.

19.04 The times indicated on the Draw Chart are for players guidance only, who should be prepared to be called up to the Control Desk up to 45 minutes earlier than the times indicated.

19.05 The BDO appointed Organisers reserve the right to seed players, or teams, in the draw for a darts event, whenever necessary.

19.06 No substitutes shall be allowed in an Individual darts event.

19.07 No substitutes shall be allowed after the first round of a team event, unless the Playing Rules of the particular event allow for reserve members of a team to be used, or in extenuating circumstances allowed for at the discretion of the BDO appointed Organisers.

20.00 Order of play

20.01 The Order of Play shall be determinated by a draw, or toss of a coin, at the Control Desk, prior to the issue of a Match Assignment Card.

20.02 The Winner of the draw, or toss, shall throw first in the first Leg, or Set, and all ODD alternate Legs, or Sets, thereafter in that respective match.

20.03 The Loser of the draw, or toss, shall throw first in the second Leg, or Set, and if applicable, in all EVEN alternate Legs, or Sets, thereafter in that respective match.

20.04 If the Order of Play has not been correctly adopted then that respective leg shall be stopped, and then restarted using the correct Order of Play.

20.05 If legs have already been completed using an incorrect Order of Play then the results determined in those legs shall stand, but the next leg shall be started using the correct Order of Play.

21.00 Match assignment/ result/record card

21.01 An assignment/result/record card shall be made out, at the Control Desk, detailing the Order of Play, and indicating the Order of Throwing. This card shall be presented to the assigned MatchBoard referee by the player, the referee shall be responsible for ensuring that the Order of Play, and Order of Throwing is strictly adhered to during that respective match.

21.02 On conclusion of the match the referee shall sign the assignment/result/record card clearly indicating the winning player and the card shall be returned immediately to the Control Desk by the winning player.

21.03 The progression of players shall be marked up on Draw Charts, or made available at the Control Desk, so that players, or spectators can determine the current positions during the darts event.

21.04 When made available, all players are required to wear ID badges at all times during a darts event, unless specifically requested to remove them by a BDO appointed Official, i.e. during a televised stage match.

22.00 Practice

22.01 Each player is ONLY entitled to '6' practice darts to be thrown at the assigned Match-Board prior to the match commencing. No other practice darts may be thrown during that match, without the prior permission, or instruction, of the MatchBoard referee.

22.02 In Round Robin events a player's practice darts shall be reduced to '3' for the second, and subsequent visits to the MatchBoard.

22.03 No practice shall be allowed on unassigned MatchBoards after the darts event has officially started.

22.04 Practice Boards shall be provided in, or adjacent to, the tournament room for the exclusive use of tournament players ONLY.

23.00 Tournament play

23.01 In tournament play all players shall play under the supervision and direction of BDO appointed Organisers and Officials.

23.02 No person shall be allowed within the Playing Area other than the MatchBoard referee, markers, scores recorders, and assigned players.

23.03 Only referees, or markers, and the DartBoard Indicator operators shall be allowed to be situated in front of a player actually at the Oche throwing darts.

23.04 Stage officials are expected to restrict their own movements to a minimum during the course of a player's throw, and they are not permitted to smoke, or drink on stage during a match.

23.05 A player's opponent must stand at least '610' mm (2 ft 0 in) to the rear of the player actually at the Oche.

23.06 In 'stage finals' the players shall engage in matchplay under the supervision and direction of Stage Officials, and in between throws shall be located in such a position as to afford an unrestricted view of proceedings for players, Officials, spectators, and in some darts events, for television/video cameras.

23.07 During matchplay all players shall remain silent, and only the player at the Oche shall direct enquiries to the referee. Neither shall any prompting be allowed by any other player, any spectator, or any Official.

23.08 Any player in breach of clause 23.07 shall first be warned by the referee in the presence of the Player's Captain, or Team Manager;

any subsequent breach during the same match shall incur the immediate disqualification of that player from that respective match.

The voicing of an enquiry, or protest, to the referee shall not constitue a breach of Clause 23.07.

23.09 A player at the Oche is entitled to consult with the referee on the amount scored, or required, at any time during a throw; however, the player shall not be advised on how to finish.

23.10 Any enquiries on scores recorded, or subtractions made, will not be entered into after the conclusion of that respective leg, set, or match.

23.11 In team events where all players throw in rotation, the Order of Throwing must be determined and displayed on the MatchBoard before the first throw of that leg, set, or match, whichever is applicable.

23.12 Any protest must be lodged with the MatchBoard referee, or Floor Controller, at the time of the alleged violation and a judgement given on the spot before the leg, set, or match is allowed to continue. Any late protests will not be honoured.

23.13 If a player's playing equipment becomes damaged, or is lost during the course of a throw then the player shall be allowed up to a maximum of three minutes in which to repair, or replace, the playing equipment.

23.14 A maximum time limit of three minutes, subject to the referee's permission, shall be allowed in the instance of a player requiring to leave the playing area, in exceptional circumstances, during the course of matchplay.

23.15 During matchplay, any players using offensive language, or seen to be 'mouthing' any offensive language, or seen to be making offensive gestures, shall be deemed to have brought the Sport of Darts into disrepute, and shall become liable to Disciplinary Proceedings being taken against them.

See BDO Code of Practice No III in the BDO Authorised Handbook.

24.00 Tie breaker

24.01 In some darts events the 'tie breaker' principle is brought into operation when the match result has reached an equality in Sets for each player, with one Set, the Final Set, remaining to be played.

The terms of the Tie Breaker Rule shall then apply to the last Leg of the Final Set of that match.

24.02 Each player shall throw for the Bull to determine which player shall throw first in the last Leg of the Final Set, but the player that threw first in the match shall throw first for the Bull.

24.03 The decision will be based on the player's dart that enters the board, remains in the board, and is judged by the referee to be nearer the Bull.

24.04 Darts that hit and remain in the Bull, or 25 bed, shall be retrieved by the player before the opponent throws a dart.

24.05 If a dart rebounds from the board, or falls out of the board during a throw, then the player shall throw a further dart, or darts, until one remains in the board.

24.06 If a dart enters, and remains in the board, in such a manner that the opponent's view of the Bull, or 25 Bed, is obscured, then the opponent may request the referee to adjust the angle of inclination of the dart so as to afford a clearer view.

Any adjustment of the angle of inclination must not alter the point of entry of the dart, but must align the dart so that it is perpendicular to the face of the board.

24.07 If the darts thrown for the Bull prove to be a tie, then both players shall retrieve their darts and shall throw again in reverse order, until a decision has been made by the referee.

24.08 The player that wins the last Leg of the Final Set is the winner of the match.

25.00 Playing attire

25.01 Players are not permitted to wear jeans, neither shall they wear trousers, or skirts made with denim, or corduroy material, which have been fashioned in a 'jeans style'.

This restriction shall also apply to any form of 'track-suit' attire.

25.02 No headgear shall be worn, without the prior permission of the BDO appointed Organisers, e.g. a Sikh would qualify for such permission.

25.03 Players are permitted to wear sweatbands on their wrists.

25.04 Players are not permitted to wear cardigans, or jumpers over their approved Playing Attire.

25.05 All players, or teams, representing their County at Regional Play-offs and Grand Finals shall wear their County approved Playing Attire, subject to meeting the requirements of Clause 25.07.

25.06 All players, or teams, representing their Country in a BDO darts event shall wear their Country approved Playing Attire, subject to meeting the requirements of Clause 25.07.

25.07 Member County, and International Member Country Organisers are recommended to have 'unmarked' Playing Attire available which shall be used on those occasions when advertising rights are likely to be infringed.

25.08 In all BDO darts events the Playing Attire of any participating player shall be subject to BDO approval.

Any unacceptable Playing Attire must be changed before that player can participate in any introductions, matchplay on stage, interviews, and presentations.

25.09 Any player refusing to meet with BDO approval shall be liable to forfeit that respective match, and shall be reported to the appropriate darts body for Disciplinary Proceedings to be considered.

See BDO code of practice No III in the BDO authorised handbook.

25.10 In Open events Clauses 25.01 to 25.09 shall not be enforced until players are required to participate in any introductions, presentations, and matchplay on stage.

26.00 Playing records

26.01 All players scores shall be recorded in the final rounds of all BDO darts events on official BDO Match Result Sheets, or Score Cards, so that reports on the darts events can be authenticated.

26.02 Such records may also be made available to Member County, and International Member Country Selection Committees for determining the suitability of players for Inter-County, or International status.

27.00 Advertising

27.01 The BDO appointed Organisers reserve the rights to the use of all advertising material, slogans, or logos, in connection with the promotion and the organisation of any BDO darts event.

27.02 The BDO appointed Organisers reserve the right to protect their Sponsor's interests with regard to any advertising material, slogans, or logos, used by players, teams, or other Sponsors, during a BDO darts event.

27.03 Players and spectators in a BDO darts event will not be allowed to wear any clothing that bears any advertising material, slogans, or logos, relating to any marketable product, or concern, without the prior written permission of the British Darts Organisation.

27.04 Players in a BDO darts event will not be allowed to use any playing equipment that bears any advertising material, slogans, or logos, relating to any marketable product, or concern, with-out the prior written permission of the British Darts Organisation.

27.05 Before any televised stage matches BDO appointed Officials, including the referee, are empowered to request a player to withdraw, or remove, any offending advertising material, slogans, or logos, which contravene any Clause in BDO Playing Rule 27, or any Television Advertising Rules currently in force at the time of the darts event.

In those instances when a player refuses to comply with such a request then that player, or team shall forfeit that match.

27.06 In those instances when a player introduces on to stage any advertising material, slogans, or logos, which contravene any Clause in BDO Playing Rule 27, or any Television Advertising Rules currently in force at the time of the darts event, then that player, or team shall forfeit that match.

28.00 Smoking

28.01 No smoking shall be allowed by any player, or match official, whilst engaged in a match played on stage which is being covered by television.

28.02 No smoking shall be allowed by any player, or match official, whilst engaged in the televised introductions to matchplay, during any televised interviews either on or off the stage, and during presentation ceremonies made on the stage.

28.03 Any player found to be in breach of Clause 28.01, or 28.02 shall be liable to forfeit that respective match, and shall be reported to the appropriate darts body for Disciplinary Proceedings to be considered.

28.04 Any match official found to be in breach of Clause 28.01, or 28.02 shall be reported to the appropriate darts body for Disciplinary Proceedings to be considered.

See BDO code of practice No III in the BDO authorised handbook.

28.05 The British Darts Organisation Ltd., or any of its subsidiaries, reserves the right to prohibit smoking in any other matches under its jurisdiction if it is considered to be in the best interests of the promotion of the Sport of Darts to do so.

29.00 Drinking

29.01 No alcoholic drinks shall be allowed to be consumed, or introduced into the area covered by television, by any player, or match official whilst engaged in a match played on stage which is being covered by television.

29.02 No alcoholic drinks shall be allowed to be consumed, or introduced into the area covered by television, by any player, or match official during televised introductions to matchplay, during any televised interviews either on or off the stage, and during presentation ceremonies made on the stage.

29.03 Any player found to be in breach of Clause 29.01, or 29.02 shall be liable to forfeit that respective match, and shall be reported to the appropriate darts body for Disciplinary Proceedings to be considered.

29.04 Any match official found to be in breach of Clause 29.01, or 29.02 shall be reported to the appropriate darts body for Disciplinary Proceedings to be considered.

See BDO code of practice No III in the BDO authorised handbook.

29.05 The British Darts Organisation Ltd., or any of its subsidiaries, shall reserve the right to prohibit the consumption of alcoholic drinks in any other matches under its jurisdiction, if it is considered to be in the best interests of the promotion of the Sport of Darts to do so.

30.00 Organisation of darts events

30.01 The British Darts Organisation Ltd., or any of its subsidiaries, shall have the right to organise a darts event anywhere in the British Isles.

Wherever possible the BDO shall endeavour to schedule darts events so as to avoid clashing with any known major darts events.

30.02 A Member County shall NOT be allowed to organise a darts event, in an area known to be under another Member County's jurisdiction, without the other Member County's involvement, or written approval.

30.03 No Member County shall organise, or promote, a 'National' titled darts event without the written authority of the Board of Directors.

30.04 A member County appointed to organise the County, or Area Play-off of a BDO darts event, which includes players from more than one Member County, shall not organise that play-off on a date allocated for the County, or Area play-off of another BDO darts event.

31.00 Exclusion

31.01 The British Darts Organisation Ltd., reserves the right to exclude any Playing Member, or Official, or Member County, or Member Country Darts Organisation from any, or all BDO Members-Only darts events, if that Playing Member, or Official, or Member County, or Member Country Darts Organisation is found to be in breach of any of the BDO Playing Rules, or any of the Rules and Regulations laid down in Volume ONE and Volume TWO of the BDO Authorised Handbook.

31.02 The exclusion of any Playing Member, or Official, or Member County, or Member Country Darts Organisation from any, or all BDO Members-Only darts events, shall ONLY be put into effect as a result of Disciplinary Proceedings being taken in accordance with BDO Code of Practice No III as laid down in the BDO Authorised Handbook.

31.03 The British Darts Organisation reserves the right to 'debt-suspend' any player, or team, or Playing Member, or Official, or Member County, or Member Country Darts Organisation from any, or all BDO darts events until such time as all outstanding debts have been cleared.

32.00 Amendments and additions

32.01 The British Darts Organisation Ltd., reserves the right to add to, or amend, any, or all, of the BDO Playing Rules, at any time to meet any purpose deemed to be necessary at that time by the Board of Directors.

33.00 Copyright

33.01 The entire contents of the BDO Playing Rules are the copyright of the British Darts Organisation Ltd., and may not be reprinted, copied, duplicated, or otherwise reproduced, wholly, or in part, without the written consent of the copyright owner.

33.02 When a darts event is being staged outside the jurisdiction of the British Darts Organisation Ltd., the Organisers of that darts event may be given consent to state that 'BDO PLAYING RULES APPLY', on entry forms, and other darts event literature.

Consent to do this can only be obtained by making application in writing to the BDO Headquarters, 2 Pages Lane, Muswell Hill, London N10 1PS.

Index